COOL MILITARY

INFORMATION SYSTEMS

JOSH GREGORY

Published in the United States of America by
Cherry Lake Publishing, Ann Arbor, Michigan
www.cherrylakepublishing.com

Content Adviser

Cynthia Watson, PhD, author of *U.S. National Security*

Credits

Cover and page 1, ©Stango/Dreamstime.com; page 4, U.S. Army photo by Georgios Moumoulidis/Released; page 6, ©ClassicStock/Alamy; page 9, U.S. Navy photo by Mass Communication Specialist 3rd Class Shawn J. Stewart/Released; pages 10, 14, and 26, U.S. Navy photo by Mass Communication Specialist 3rd Class Christopher K. Hwang/Released; page 12, U.S. Marine Corps photo by Lance Cpl. James Frazer/Released; page 16, U.S. Air Force photo by Master Sgt. Matthew Lohr/Released; page 18, U.S. Marine Corps photo by Lance Cpl. Marco Mancha/Released; page 21, ©ASSOCIATED PRESS; page 23, ©Gina Rodgers/Alamy; page 24, U.S. Marine Corps Photo by Lance Cpl. Andres J. Lugo/Released; page 29, U.S. Navy photo by Gary Nichols/Released.

Library of Congress Cataloging-in-Publication Data

Gregory, Josh.
 Information systems technician/by Josh Gregory.
     p. cm.—(Cool military careers) (21st century skills)
 Includes bibliographical references and index.
 Audience: Grades 4-6.
 ISBN 978-1-61080-447-9 (lib. bdg.) — ISBN 978-1-61080-534-6 (e-book) —
ISBN 978-1-61080-621-3 (pbk.)
 1. United States—Armed Forces—Data processing—Juvenile literature.
2. Information technology—Vocational guidance—Juvenile literature. I. Title.
 UA23.G83 2012
 355.3'4—dc23   2012001722

Cherry Lake Publishing would like to acknowledge
the work of The Partnership for 21st Century Skills.
Please visit *www.21stcenturyskills*.org for more information.

Printed in the United States of America
Corporate Graphics Inc.
July 2012
CLFA11

COOL MILITARY CAREERS

TABLE OF CONTENTS

CHAPTER ONE

COMPUTERS IN THE MILITARY

Sam was playing a video game on his computer when his mom walked past, carrying a basket of laundry. She slowed down as the computer monitor caught her eye. "What are you up to?" she asked.

Computers are an important part of today's military operations.

"Just playing on the computer," Sam answered.

"Well, I can see that much!" his mom replied. "What are you doing in the game?"

"I'm fighting a war against bad guys from another country," he responded.

"Looks like fun," she said.

"It is!" Sam answered. "I wish it could be my job when I get older."

"Using computers or fighting wars?" Sam's mom asked.

Sam thought about the question for a moment and then answered with excitement. "Both!" he shouted.

"Believe it or not," she said, "there is a way you can do that."

■ ■ ■

Like most businesses and government organizations today, all five branches of the U.S. military rely heavily on computer systems to manage their day-to-day activities. The military uses computers for basic tasks such as accounting, scheduling, and record keeping. It also uses them for more specialized purposes such as controlling weapons systems and collecting and analyzing **intelligence**.

The Internet and other smaller **networks** allow military personnel to communicate with each other from anywhere in the world. Computer networks have become such a necessary part of military operations that it is difficult to remember a time when they weren't used. It wasn't very long ago, however, that the military was fighting major wars without computers.

Around the time of World War II (1939–1945), computers were still new inventions. The computers that existed then were much different from the ones we use today. Modern

Early computers took up entire rooms and were less powerful than modern cell phones.

computers, such as smartphones, are often small enough to fit in your pants pocket. Early computers, however, were huge—a single computer filled an entire large room.

LIFE & CAREER SKILLS

In 1958, the U.S. Department of Defense organized a new government agency called the Defense Advanced Research Projects Agency. Its purpose was to ensure that the United States stayed on the cutting edge of technology. One of its earliest projects was to create a **secure** network for sending information between computer systems. As time went on, smaller networks were combined to form larger ones. As the process grew, computers at government and military offices were connected to research laboratories at universities. The network eventually grew to become the Internet that we know today. What began as a military experiment ended up being one of the most important inventions in history. Working for the military gives you the chance to work on projects that could change the world.

These gigantic computers were used mainly for working with numbers in important government projects. They were much less powerful than even the simplest computers we have today. In the following years, computer technology began to advance at an incredible rate. Military leaders soon recognized the many potential uses computers could have in fighting wars and defending the United States.

At the same time, computer **hardware** was becoming smaller and more powerful, just as it continues to do today. In the late 1970s, the first personal computers were manufactured for public use. They were much smaller than the **mainframes** that were used by businesses and government organizations. This made them easy to move from place to place. Suddenly, it was possible to set up a computer network almost anywhere.

Nearly all businesses and organizations today, including the U.S. military, employ information systems technicians to maintain their computers and networks. These skilled experts are often referred to as information technology (IT) workers. Their works ensures that the computer systems of the U.S. Army, Navy, Air Force, Marine Corps, and Coast Guard will always be functional when they are needed.

Information systems technicians help build and maintain communications systems wherever the military needs them.

CHAPTER TWO
ANOTHER DAY AT THE OFFICE

M any jobs in the military are not much different from **civilian** jobs. Whether working in the offices of a major corporation or aboard a U.S. Navy submarine off the coast of a faraway country, IT workers have many of the same responsibilities.

Whether working for the military or a civilian company, IT workers do similar tasks.

One of their main duties is to design, install, and maintain computer networks. This requires them to work with hardware, **software**, and **peripherals**. Hardware consists of the actual parts that make up a computer, such as hard drives, memory, or the central processing unit (CPU). The CPU is the portion of a computer that carries out the instructions of a computer program. IT workers need to understand how each part functions, why it is important, and how it affects the other parts of the computer.

Software is another term for the programs that run on a computer and allow it to complete different tasks. Peripherals are devices that are attached to computers to give them new uses. They include everything from printers and speakers to the high-tech cameras and sensors the military uses to gather intelligence.

IT workers create networks by assembling hardware, installing software, and attaching any necessary peripherals. Then they connect them together using devices such as **modems** and **routers**.

The level of security on civilian networks varies greatly. It's often easy for hackers or viruses to attack a home computer network, but large businesses usually have better security systems. Because the information they deal with can be a matter of national security, military networks have some of the strongest security in the world. IT workers use a variety of hardware and software solutions to prevent enemies from stealing information or otherwise harming military networks.

Any time there's a problem with a computer, IT workers are called in to solve it. They use their knowledge to **troubleshoot** and discover the source of the problem. Then they figure out a solution, which could include replacing a piece of hardware or changing the settings in a program. IT workers need to be able to think fast and solve problems as quickly as possible. Military operations are often based on strict schedules.

IT workers often instruct other members of the military on how to use their computers and solve common issues.

Some IT workers specialize in compiling and managing data. The military keeps detailed records of its employees, resources, and finances. IT workers are responsible for creating and maintaining databases to organize this information. These databases allow other military workers to quickly access the information they need to do their jobs.

LEARNING & INNOVATION SKILLS

IT workers must always be knowledgeable about the latest technology. Because technology advances so rapidly, keeping up-to-date on new developments can seem like a full-time second job. IT workers read Web sites and magazines that report on new technology. Sometimes workers take classes to learn about the latest hardware or software. Without this extra education, an IT worker's knowledge of technology would quickly become dated.

Highly experienced IT workers are often given advanced tasks that make full use of their valuable skills. They perform research and decide which computer equipment will be most beneficial to the military. Then they work with technology companies to find the best prices for new equipment. They also work with experts to design new hardware and software when the military needs something that does not yet exist.

Information systems technicians find ways to use new technology to improve military operations.

Experienced IT workers are responsible for training and supervising new workers, as well.

Even though their duties are very similar to those of civilian IT workers, military IT workers often do their jobs in a variety of unusual environments. Some work aboard ships or submarines. Others set up new networks on temporary military bases in foreign nations. Some work in offices or military bases on home soil.

IT workers follow the basic patterns of military life. They wake up early in the morning and work throughout the day. They must exercise regularly to stay in good shape, and they must learn to follow orders from their superiors. And they must always be prepared for danger. IT workers usually do their jobs indoors, away from the front lines, but any military site is a potential target for attack. These things can make military IT jobs much more stressful and difficult than civilian ones.

CHAPTER THREE

BECOMING AN INFORMATION SYSTEMS TECHNICIAN

D espite the difficult times you might face in the armed forces, the military offers many benefits that no other job can provide. It's important to weigh the positive and

Before joining the military, consider whether you are willing to live and work in faraway nations.

negative aspects of the job when deciding whether or not to pursue a career in the military. It's always a good idea to talk with family and friends before making the decision to join. **Recruiters** can also provide information and answer any questions you might have.

LIFE & CAREER SKILLS

Studying textbooks and taking classes aren't the only ways to learn important job skills. You probably have most of the things you need to begin learning about computers and networks in your home already. All you need to get started is a computer and an Internet connection. If you don't have a computer at home, you can use one at your school or local public library. Spend time learning about different hardware, software, programming languages, and networks. The Internet itself is a useful resource for obtaining this kind of information. Many of the world's most famous computer experts, including Microsoft's Bill Gates and Apple's Steve Jobs, learned a lot about how computers work by studying on their own. In many cases, they actually built the first computers they worked on!

Once you've decided to join the military, you must determine which branch is the right one for you. IT jobs are very similar from branch to branch. However, there are still important differences to consider. Each branch has bases and other facilities in different parts of the world. Joining the Navy makes you more likely to be stationed aboard a ship or a submarine, since the Navy does much of its work at sea. Coast

Like all members of the military, information systems technicians must stay in good physical shape.

Guard IT workers are more likely to work in the United States, since the Coast Guard operates mainly in the waters close to home.

If you want to become a military IT worker, it's a good idea to begin preparing as early as possible. Classes in computer science or programming will help you learn the basic skills of the job. Math and science classes are also very helpful. You might even want to practice building your own computers and designing your own programs. These skills will be useful in a wide range of technology careers.

In addition to technical knowledge, military IT workers should be organized. They often need to keep track of complicated information, so having things well organized and easy to find helps them be more efficient. IT workers should also have a keen eye for details. Sometimes a very small error can cause huge problems in a computer system. Finally, they should be able to think creatively when it comes to solving problems. Often there is no simple answer to solving a computer problem. The problem might even be something that's never happened before. In these types of situations, IT workers must think of new, original ways to find solutions.

There are certain traits that all members of the military share. They must be willing to follow orders and work long days doing difficult tasks. They must also be willing to work as part of a team with other military personnel, without allowing personal feelings about other people stand in the way.

There are two general categories of military employees: officers and enlisted personnel. Officers are the leaders of the military. They have college degrees and are usually placed in charge of more advanced tasks. Enlisted personnel make up the majority of the military. They do not need college degrees, though many have taken at least some college classes. Most IT workers are enlisted personnel, though there are plenty of officers with IT-related jobs.

To become an enlisted member of the military, you sign up with a recruiter. All branches of the armed forces have recruiting offices throughout the country. Recruiters also visit high school and job fairs to find people who would be a good fit for the military. Candidates wishing to enlist take a test called the Armed Services Vocational Aptitude Battery (ASVAB). It tests their knowledge in a range of different subjects and shows which careers would suit them best.

After enlisting, new recruits attend basic training. This program lasts several weeks and prepares newly enlisted personnel for life in the military. During basic training, the new recruits participate in a variety of physical drills and exercises. It can be extremely difficult for people who are out of shape, so it helps to begin training on your own before joining the military.

Once basic training is over, those interested in IT and who have gotten good marks on the ASVAB attend an additional training program. There they learn the skills they'll need to

Recruiters can answer any questions you might have about joining the military.

build and maintain the military's computer networks. The exact length of these programs is different for each branch. At 25 weeks, the Coast Guard's program is the longest. The Air Force program lasts only eight and a half weeks. No matter the length, each program covers roughly the same topics. Trainees spend time taking classes and getting hands-on experience with everything from network security to programming languages.

Becoming an officer is a different process from enlisting. There are several paths to officer jobs, and each requires a college degree. First, a person can attend one of the U.S. military colleges, such as the U.S. Military Academy in West Point, New York; the U.S. Naval Academy in Annapolis, Maryland; or the Coast Guard Academy in New London, Connecticut. Students at these schools major in subjects of their choosing while receiving military training. Admission to each is very competitive, but all students become officers in the U.S. military upon graduation.

Students at civilian colleges can become officers by joining the Reserve Officers' Training Corps (ROTC). They participate in drills and training exercises while also working toward degrees. In return, they usually receive **scholarships**. Like graduates of U.S. military colleges, ROTC graduates become officers after finishing school. College graduates with no military training can also become officers. To do so, they must attend officer candidate school for the branch of their choosing.

West Point and other military academy students become officers after graduating.

CHAPTER FOUR
WHAT COMES NEXT?

The U.S. military is usually in need of hardworking men and women to fill its many jobs. When it is, all you need to do is

Even when there is a waiting list, strong computer skills can help you find a place in the military.

enlist and make it through basic training. Since the early 2000s, however, more people have wanted to enlist than the military has needed. As a result, many people have been placed on a waiting list. In these situations, having college credit or useful skills such as computer knowledge can help against the competition.

21ST CENTURY CONTENT

Civilian IT workers will have many job opportunities in the future. The U.S. Bureau of Labor Statistics predicts that the number of jobs will grow much faster in the IT field than in most other fields over the next several years. As of 2008, most jobs in the civilian IT industry paid between $54,000 and $84,000 per year. The top 10 percent of IT workers earn more than $110,000. If you're considering a job in the military, it's never too early to think about what you might want to do after retiring. Military service can prepare you for an excellent civilian job, if you plan properly and train in related fields.

It is nearly impossible to predict how many more workers the military will require in the future. Its needs vary depending on whether the nation is at war, what types of strategies are being used to fight wars, and how many people are trying to enlist at the time. Politics and world events are constantly changing, so the military can find itself with too many employees one day and a shortage the next.

As technology advances, information systems technicians will continue to play an important role in the military.

The military's base pay rates depends on a person's **rank** and years of experience. These pay rates are the same for all five branches and increase slightly every year. As of 2012, enlisted personnel earn anywhere from about $18,000 to $75,000 a year. Officers earn more than enlisted personnel. Their salaries range between $34,000 and about $225,000.

Military employees are eligible to receive a variety of benefit payments in addition to their base salaries. Hazardous duty pay is awarded to those who are sent to work in dangerous areas, such as war zones. Men and women who are sent to faraway nations can earn foreign duty pay. Bonuses are also awarded to those who have special skills needed by the military. These might include being able to use specialized computer equipment or being able to speak a foreign language.

Another benefit of working for the military is that all members are provided with free housing on military bases, free meals, and free clothing. Those who don't live on military bases are eligible to receive allowances to help cover their living expenses.

The military allows its members to retire after 20 years of service. Many people first join the military when they are in their late teens or early 20s. This means they can retire from military duty while they are still young enough to begin new careers. They can pursue new jobs, further their educations, or work toward achieving other goals while continuing to collect paychecks from the military. The armed forces offer a variety of scholarships for former members who want to attend college. The military also provides career services to help them find new jobs.

There are many civilian careers that are well suited to former military IT workers. These workers can find jobs as programmers, network administrators, or software designers for civilian companies. There are many private companies in the world, and almost all of them employ a variety of computer and network experts. They may require additional training after leaving the military to be qualified for these jobs. However, their military IT training often counts as college credit, which speeds up the process of earning any degrees they might need.

As technology continues its rapid advances, it will likely play an even large role in our lives than it currently does. The U.S. military will be among the countless organizations looking for skilled professionals to maintain computers and networks. With enough hard work, you could be one of those professionals one day. Are you up to the challenge?

Will you join the military and become an information systems technician?

GLOSSARY

civilian (suh-VIL-yuhn) not part of the military

hardware (HAHRD-wair) computer equipment, such as hard drives and memory

intelligence (in-TEL-uh-juhnts) information gathered and used by government agencies to plan and make important decisions

mainframes (MAYN-fraimz) large, powerful computers that help run smaller computers

modems (MOH-duhmz) electronic devices that allow computers to exchange data

networks (NET-wurks) groups of connected computers or communications equipment

peripherals (puh-RIF-ur-uhlz) external devices, such as printers or modems, that are connected to and controlled by computers

rank (RANGK) an official job level or position

recruiters (ri-KROO-turz) military employees in charge of signing up new members and providing information to people who are interested in joining the military

routers (RAUT-urz) devices that handle signals between computers or computer networks

scholarships (SKAHL-ur-ships) money given to pay for college or follow a course of study

secure (si-KYOOR) safe, trustworthy

software (SAWFT-wair) computer programs that control the workings of the hardware and direct it to do specific tasks

troubleshoot (TRUH-buhl-shoot) to use specialized knowledge to determine the cause of and solution to a problem

FOR MORE INFORMATION

BOOKS

Freedman, Jeri. *Careers in Computer Science and Programming.* New York: Rosen Publishing Group, 2011.

Graham, Ian. *Technology Careers.* Mankato, MN: Amicus, 2011.

Kiland, Taylor Baldwin. *The U.S. Navy and Military Careers.* Berkeley Heights, NJ: Enslow Publishers, 2006

WEB SITES

America's Navy—Information Technology
www.navy.com/careers/information-and-technology/information-technology.html
Read more about the duties of Navy IT workers.

Bureau of Labor Statistics—Occupational Outlook Handbook: Network and Computer Systems Administrators
www.bls.gov/oco/ocos305.htm
Find out more about civilian IT jobs.

U.S. Army—Careers & Jobs: Information Technology Specialist
www.goarmy.com/careers-and-jobs/browse-career-and-job-categories/computers-and-technology/information-technology-specialist.html
Learn more about becoming an Army IT worker.

INDEX

ABOUT THE AUTHOR

Josh Gregory writes and edits books for kids. He lives in Chicago, Illinois.